# Contents

D0495283

# My Exam Reviser

### What is the Exam Reviser?

The Exam Reviser contains language and advice relevant to the Cambridge FCE exam. It is organised in a way that means you can easily find summaries of different areas of language, as well as advice about the exam itself.

The main vocabulary from each of the Coursebook units is summarised in the **Vocabulary** section. There is also additional vocabulary linked to some of the topics.

In the **Functional Language** section you will find useful phrases for both the speaking and writing parts of the exam.

There are also sections on common **Phrasal Verbs** (including example sentences) and **Useful Language Chunks** (e.g. *it takes ages, there's no point in*, etc.).

The **Top Tips for the Exam** section includes advice for each of the five papers in the exam. The last section, **My Exam**, is designed to help you plan your revision time.

### How and when should I use it?

As you work through the Coursebook in class, you will notice references to the Exam Reviser, particularly for the **Vocabulary** and **Functional Language** sections. Sometimes, you will be asked to do something in the Exam Reviser, e.g. to complete a table with more words and phrases, or to write some example sentences. At other times, there is nothing to write, but you should still take time to look at the relevant sections. By the end of the course, your Exam Reviser will provide you with a completed summary of the language you need for the exam.

As you get nearer the date of your exam, have a look at the **My Exam** section and use **My revision timetable** to organise your revision time, making sure you know the date, time and place of each paper. Check that you have read and understood the information in the **Top Tips for the Exam** section, too.

In the last couple of weeks before your exam, you can use your Exam Reviser to help you revise different aspects of language – using the completed **Vocabulary** and **Functional Language** sections, and the sections on **Phrasal Verbs** and **Useful Language Chunks**. You could set yourself targets, e.g. to learn ten words and phrases from a particular section each day, or to test a friend on a particular section. Don't forget to look at, and if necessary update, **My revision timetable** as the days go by.

In the last two or three days before the exam, keep your Exam Reviser with you. Use it to test yourself and your friends in spare moments, e.g. on the bus or while you're having breakfast!

On the day before your exam, check again that you know the time and place of the exam. Look at the **Top Tips for the Exam** one more time and then have an early night!

On the day of your exam, put your Exam Reviser away. You have now done as much as you can. Try to relax and enjoy the exam! Good luck!

# Vocabulary

## Unit 1 | Entertain me

### 1.1 Going out  coursebook  p8

| Types of music | Types of film | Things you can see in a theatre or concert hall | Things you can see in a museum or art gallery |
|---|---|---|---|
| jazz | horror film | a play | sculpture |
| soul | science fiction film | a concert | paintings |
| heavy metal | comedy film | a ballet | drawings |
| classical music | action adventure | a show | modern art |
| dance music | film | a musical | historical objects |
| | period drama | | |

### 1.2 Staying in  coursebook  p13

| Things you can read | Things you can do on a computer | Types of TV programmes | Things to do with friends at home |
|---|---|---|---|
| novel | download music | soap (opera) | to have friends round (for a meal) |
| autobiography | shop online | documentary | |
| biography | send emails | chat show | to go round to a friend's (for a meal) |
| non-fiction | receive emails | sports programme | |
| fiction | play computer | quiz show | to have a barbecue |
| newspaper (tabloid/ | games | news | to have a party |
| quality) | write and edit | current affairs | to have a dinner |
| magazine | documents | programme | party |
| scientific journal | view and edit | a drama series | to invite someone in |
| | photographs | a sitcom | for coffee |

# Unit 2 | Family and friends

## 2.1 Family and relationships `coursebook` `p17`

| Male | | Female | |
|------|------|--------|------|
| father | partner | mother | partner |
| step-father | boyfriend | step-mother | girlfriend |
| brother | fiancé | sister | fiancée |
| half-brother | husband | half-sister | wife |
| step-brother | husband-to-be | step-sister | wife-to-be |
| son | ex-boyfriend | daughter | ex-girlfriend |
| cousin | ex-husband | cousin | ex-wife |
| uncle | | aunt | |
| grandfather | friend | grandmother | friend |
| father-in-law | best friend | mother-in-law | best friend |
| brother-in-law | acquaintance | sister-in-law | acquaintance |
| | colleague | | colleague |
| classmate | flatmate | classmate | flatmate |
| flatmate | | flatmate | |

## 2.2 Describing people `coursebook` `p24`

| Hair | Build | General appearance |
|------|-------|--------------------|
| blond | slim | well-dressed |
| curly | well-built | smart |
| shoulder-length | stocky | in her mid-30s |
| clean-shaven | | |
| a beard | | |

# Unit 3 | Lifestyles

## 3.1 Places to live  coursebook  p27

| Places to live | Definitions |
|---|---|
| detached house | A a riverboat that you can live on |
| semi-detached house | B a house with only one floor (no upstairs) |
| terraced house | C a small house in the country or in a village |
| flat | D a house joined at one side to another house |
| block of flats | E a house not joined to any other house |
| maisonette | F a place to live which is part of a larger building (AmE: *apartment*) |
| cottage | G a large building with many flats in it (AmE: *apartment block*) |
| bungalow | H a house joined to several other houses to form a row |
| bedsit | I a place to live/stay made of cloth supported by poles and ropes |
| houseboat | J a flat with its own front entrance (usually part of a converted house) |
| tent | K a place to live in a building which used to have a different use (e.g. a barn, a garage, a church, etc.) |
| converted church | L a very small flat with a bedroom and living room in the same room |

## 3.2 At home  coursebook  p30

| Rooms and places at a home | | Machines and objects at home | |
|---|---|---|---|
| living room/lounge | utility room | washing machine | kettle |
| dining room | hall | tumble dryer | toaster |
| kitchen | landing | dishwasher | sink/basin |
| (main) bedroom | cellar/basement | fridge | bath |
| spare bedroom | conservatory | freezer | shower |
| bathroom | patio/deck | cooker/oven | toilet |
| study/office | balcony | grill | hairdryer |
| attic/loft | | microwave | iron |
| | | | ironing board |

## 3.3 Town and country  coursebook  p34

| Facilities in town | Problems in a town |
|---|---|
| police station | pollution |
| swimming pool | traffic jams |
| leisure centre/sports centre | overcrowding |
| library | vandalism |
| concert hall | graffiti |
| museum | crime |
| car park | |
| bus/train station | |

# Unit 4 | Get away from it all

## 4.1 Travel and transport coursebook p41

| Car | Train | Plane | Ship |
|-----|-------|-------|------|
| chauffeur | | | |

## 4.2 Synonyms coursebook p44

| a journey | an argument | interested | unhappy | surprised |
|-----------|-------------|------------|---------|-----------|
| expedition | quarrel | spellbound | fed up | stunned |
| excursion | row | fascinated | depressed | shocked |
| trip | dispute | intrigued | upset | amazed |

# Unit 5 | Play to win

## 5.1 Sports  coursebook  p47

| do | play | go |
|---|---|---|
| archery | snooker | hang-gliding |
| | | |

## 5.2 Success  coursebook  p51

| Verb | Noun |
|---|---|
| to succeed (in doing something) | success |
| to achieve (something, e.g. top marks) | achievement |
| to win (something, e.g. a race, a prize) | winning |
| to beat (someone) | – |
| to take (an exam, test, etc.) | – |
| to pass (an exam, test, etc.) | a pass |
| to fail (an exam, test, etc.) | a fail/failure |
| to earn (money/a living) | earnings |
| to gain (something, e.g. experience, control, weight) | gain |

# Unit 6 | Put it down to experience

## 6.1 Ages and stages   coursebook   p59

| Stages of life | |
| --- | --- |
| go to primary school | live with a friend/flatmate |
| go to secondary school | live together (with a partner) |
| have a 'coming-of-age' party/ceremony | get your first job |
| leave school | get engaged |
| graduate from university | get married |
| learn to drive | have children |
| move out (of your parents' house) | have grandchildren |
| | retire |

## 6.2 Prepositions   coursebook   p63

I'm **preparing for** the First Certificate exam in June.

1 _____.

2 _____.

3 _____.

4 _____.

5 _____.

6 _____.

## 6.3 Clothes   coursebook   p65

| Types of clothes | Parts of clothes | Ways of describing clothes | Materials that clothes are made of |
| --- | --- | --- | --- |
| suit | sleeves | short-sleeved | cotton |
| jacket | zip | loose | silk |
| trousers | collar | tight | wool |
| skirt | hem | baggy | polyester |
| shirt | buttons | close-fitting | lycra |
| t-shirt | belt | long-sleeved | denim |
| dress | cuff | sleeveless | leather |
| sweater | buckle | v-neck | velvet |
| cardigan | lining | round-neck | suede |
| hooded top | | smart | |
| shorts | | scruffy | |
| coat | | trendy | |
| trainers | | | |
| boots | | | |
| socks | | | |
| vest | | | |

# Unit 7 | Science fact, science fiction

## 7.1 Science, inventions and discoveries  coursebook  p69

| Verb | Noun | Adjective | Adverb |
|---|---|---|---|
| to discover | a discovery | – | – |
| to invent | an invention | – | – |
| – | science | scientific | scientifically |
| – | technology | technological | technologically |
| to experiment | an experiment | experimental | experimentally |
| to know | knowledge | knowledgeable | knowledgeably |
| to theorise | a theory | theoretical | theoretically |
| to analyse | analysis | analytical | analytically |

## 7.2 Alternatives to *very*  coursebook  p72

1 It was a *bitterly* cold day.
2 Living conditions are *exceedingly* harsh in the mountains.
3 My grandparents are *utterly* devoted to each other.
4 The view from here is *breathtakingly* beautiful.
5 He was *blissfully* unaware that he'd missed the deadline.
6 A lot of *fabulously* wealthy people live in this street.
7 Her new TV sitcom is *hilariously* funny.
8 It's *notoriously* difficult to park in the town centre.

# Unit 8 | Food for thought

## 8.1 Restaurants  coursebook   p81

We had a lovely *three-course meal.*
*For starters*, I had smoked salmon.
*The main course* cost about £12.
This restaurant has got some delicious *desserts.*

Could I have *the menu* please?
Could we have *the bill* please?
The *set menu* costs £10 for two *courses.*

The food has improved since the new *cook* took over.
I'm working as a *waiter* in a local café for the summer.
*The service* is very slow in that new Japanese restaurant.

Excuse me. This *plate/bowl/knife/fork/spoon/glass/cup/napkin* is dirty.
Could I have another one, please?

## 8.2 Describing and preparing food  coursebook   p82

| Ways of describing food | Ways of preparing food |
| --- | --- |
| tasty | to roast |

## 8.3 Food  coursebook   p82

| Fruits and vegetables | Meat and fish | Dairy products | Desserts and sweet food |
| --- | --- | --- | --- |
| banana | beef | milk | chocolate cake |
| orange | sausage | cheese | ice cream |
| cabbage | salmon | butter | biscuit |
| potato | sardine | yogurt | apple pie |
| carrot | | | |

# Unit 9 | The world around us

## 9.1 Environment coursebook p89

| Environmental problems | Geographical features | Natural disasters | Animals |
|---|---|---|---|
| pollution | jungle | earthquake | lion |
| greenhouse effect | beach | flood | elephant |
| ozone layer | cliff | drought | buffalo |
| global warming | mountain | famine | leopard |
| | volcano | | rhino |
| | forest | | |
| | stream | | |
| | ocean | | |
| | coast | | |
| | river | | |

## 9.2 Weather coursebook p93

| rain | wind | temperature | snow/ice | other |
|---|---|---|---|---|
| pouring with rain | strong wind | warm | frost | cloudy |
| light drizzle | gentle breeze | humid | | thick fog |
| showers | | freezing cold | | unbroken sunshine |
| | | chilly | | storm |
| | | | | thunder and lightning |

## 9.3 Adjectives: extending your range of vocabulary coursebook p94 and p107

| funny | exciting | interesting | surprising | boring | strange |
|---|---|---|---|---|---|
| amusing | gripping | fascinating | extraordinary | dull | weird |
| hilarious | nail-biting | intriguing | unbelievable | tedious | odd |
| entertaining | inspiring | thought-provoking | remarkable | monotonous | bizarre |

# Unit 10 | Talk, don't talk

## 10.1 Phrasal verbs (speaking) coursebook p100

1  It's a big room so you'll need to *speak up*.
2  My boss spends his whole time *talking down to* me.
3  I've spent the whole morning on the phone trying to *get through* to someone.
4  *Pass on* my congratulations to them.
5  He *gets his point across* clearly.
6  It was good to see so many people *speaking out* about all the new parking restrictions around here.
7  I just *picked it up* while I was living in Spain.
8  I find it so hard to *bring up* a subject like money.

## 10.2 Ways of speaking coursebook p105

| object to something | *I object to people talking loudly on their mobile phones on buses.* |
| --- | --- |
| boast about something | |
| grumble about something | |
| moan about something | |
| mumble about something | |
| mutter about something | |
| insist on something | |
| exaggerate about something | |

# Unit 11 | Cash in hand

## 11.1 Money  coursebook  p114

| Shopping | Work | Others |
|---|---|---|
| get a receipt | earn a salary | save |
| get a refund | get paid overtime | invest |
| get a discount | get a pension | lend |
| get a bargain | pay (income) tax | borrow |
| get a freebie | get paid on commission | owe |
| pay a deposit | | be in debt |
| pay the balance | | donate |
| bid for something in an auction | | inherit |
| haggle | | squander |
| | | gamble |
| pay in cash | | pay a fare |
| pay by credit card | | pay a fine |
| a £1 coin | | pay a fee |
| a £10 note | | pay rent |
| change | | leave a tip |
| the sales | | take out insurance |
| | | make a claim |
| | | be able to afford |

## 11.2 Numbers  coursebook  p116

**A**

| 1.6 | one point six |
|---|---|
| 16 | sixteen |
| 162 | one hundred and sixty-two |
| 1,625 | one thousand, six hundred and twenty-five |
| 16,255 | sixteen thousand, two hundred and fifty-five |
| 162,558 | one hundred and sixty two thousand, five hundred and fifty-eight |
| 1,625,589 | one million, six hundred and twenty five thousand, five hundred and eighty-nine |
| £6.25 | six pounds twenty-five (pence) |
| £2,349.50 | two thousand, three hundred and forty-nine pounds fifty (pence) |

Go to page 14 for 11.2 B

**B**

| 3.2% | three point two per cent |
|------|--------------------------|
| 65 kg | sixty-five kilos |
| 07739 456997 | oh double seven three nine, four five six double nine seven |
| 27°C | twenty seven degrees Celsius |
| 120 kph | a hundred and twenty kilometres per hour |
| 2 L | two litres |
| 17 km | seventeen kilometres |
| ½ | a half |
| 20.05.83 | the twentieth of May (nineteen) eighty-three |
| 0.5 | nought point five |
| £5.50 | five pounds fifty |
| 7.15 a.m. | seven fifteen a.m. (quarter past seven a.m.) |

# Unit 12 | Does crime really pay?

## 12.1 Crime and punishment coursebook p121

| Verbs | Crimes | Other nouns |
|---|---|---|
| to commit a crime | murder | a criminal |
| to be against the law | manslaughter | a jury |
| to arrest/to be arrested | burglary | a judge |
| to catch a criminal | mugging | a defence lawyer |
| to plead (not) guilty | shoplifting | a prosecution lawyer |
| to be found guilty/innocent (of …) | vandalism | an eyewitness |
| to be sentenced | joyriding | a serious offender |
| to reach a verdict | rape | a first-time offender |
| to get time off for good behaviour | kidnapping | a previous conviction |
| to be put in jail/prison | blackmail | community service |
| to be on probation | smuggling | (forensic) evidence |
| to pay a fine | drug-trafficking | a trial |
| to be released | drink-driving | a law court |

## 12.2 Phrasal verbs (crime) coursebook p126

1 *make (something) up* = invent
2 *let (someone) off* = release with little or no punishment
3 *break into* = enter illegally or by force
4 *get away with (something)* = escape
5 *own up (to something)* = admit
6 *take in/to be taken in by someone* = deceive
7 *make off with (something)* = steal and take something with you
8 *tie (someone) up* = fasten rope, etc. around someone so they cannot move or escape
9 *fight (someone) off* = stop someone doing something by fighting them
10 *set on (someone)* = make a sudden and unexpected physical attack

# Unit 13 | Weird and wonderful

## 13.1 Mysteries  coursebook  p131

| Verbs | Verbs | Adjectives |
|---|---|---|
| a mystery | to solve a mystery/puzzle/problem | mysterious |
| a magician | to work out the answer | puzzling |
| a magic trick | to find a solution | bizarre |
| an illusionist | to do/perform a magic trick | weird |
| an optical illusion | | strange |
| a mirage | | creepy |
| a (cryptic) crossword | | full of suspense |
| a (jigsaw) puzzle | | |
| a treasure hunt | | |
| a 'Whodunnit' | | |
| a haunted house | | |
| a ghost | | |

## 13.2 Feelings  coursebook  p138

| happy | sad | angry | surprised |
|---|---|---|---|
| elated | distraught | irritated | staggered |
| thrilled (to bits) | downhearted | annoyed | amazed |
| cheerful | traumatised | furious | astonished |
| pleased | miserable | in a rage | stunned |
| overjoyed | upset | | |

| frightened | worried | excited | other common feelings |
|---|---|---|---|
| scared | anxious | enthusiastic | relieved |
| terrified | nervous | exhilarated | overwhelmed |
| petrified | apprehensive | inspired | ashamed |
| scared stiff | uneasy | | embarrassed |
| | | | frustrated |

# Unit 14 | Work to live

## 14.1 Jobs and work  coursebook  p141

| Jobs | doctor<br>surgeon<br>nurse<br>midwife<br>dentist<br>physiotherapist<br>social worker<br>ambulance driver<br>teacher<br>caretaker<br>child-minder<br>librarian | university lecturer<br>research scientist<br>lawyer<br>vet<br>farmer<br>chef<br>waiter<br>architect<br>designer<br>builder<br>engineer<br>plumber | director<br>investment banker<br>clerk<br>administrator<br>receptionist<br>secretary<br>personnel officer<br>economist<br>sales rep<br>sales assistant<br>flight attendant<br>pilot | taxi driver<br>mechanic<br>cashier<br>cleaner<br>police officer<br>fire-fighter<br>pop star<br>musician<br>footballer |
|---|---|---|---|---|
| Qualities and skills | be flexible<br>be self-motivated<br>be open-minded<br>be ambitious<br>be enthusiastic<br>be hard-working | have initiative<br>be able to think on your feet<br>keep calm under pressure<br>have an eye for detail<br>be good with people | | be a good listener<br>work well in a team<br>be a team-player<br>be good with figures<br>have leadership qualities |
| Verb phrases | to work nine-to-five<br>to work flexi-time<br>to get the sack<br>to be made redundant<br>to be on maternity leave<br>to be on sick leave | to be in a dead-end job<br>to have a promising career ahead<br>to have a demanding job<br>to have a high-powered job<br>to be promoted to<br>to be headhunted for | | |

## 14.2 Phrasal verbs (work)  coursebook  p147

1  The government needs to *bring down* the level of inflation urgently.

2  We have three candidates for the new job *lined up* to see you this afternoon.

3  We've decided to *put off* our usual Tuesday staff meeting until Friday because so many people are off sick.

4  Steve finally *turned up* nearly twenty minutes after the presentation had started.

5  We really must *cut back* on travel expenses. From now on, all junior managers must fly economy class.

6  Our local big supermarket has *branched out* into selling designer jeans and t-shirts.

7  Why does she want to leave? We only *took* her *on* in March.

8  Who do you think will *take over* as manager when Sue goes on maternity leave?

9  You know you can always *count on* Jamie in a crisis.

10  Apparently, due to falling demand EngCom have *laid off* another 300 workers.

# Unit 15 | State of mind

## 15.1 Memory coursebook p151

1 I can't *remember* what time the meeting starts.
2 She *forgets* my birthday every year!
3 I'm much more *forgetful* than I used to be.
4 He's got a really *good memory for* phone numbers.
5 I need to *revise* for my exam next week.
6 Will you *remind me to* phone Jack later?
7 This song really *reminds me of* last summer.
8 I sometimes use rhymes to *jog my memory* about difficult spellings.
9 He's very good at *learning* song lyrics *by heart*.
10 When I play the piano, I prefer to play *from memory*.
11 I love acting, but I find *memorising* the words very difficult.
12 We had a really *memorable* day out with all the family.
13 Seeing those old school photos made me feel quite *nostalgic*.
14 My grandmother loves *reminiscing* with her sister about their childhood.

## 15.2 Idioms with *mind* coursebook p158

1 She looks terrible. She's obviously got something *on her mind*.
2 It never *crossed my mind* that he wasn't a real sales rep.
3 *My mind went blank* and I just couldn't remember her name.
4 I'm finding it difficult to *keep my mind on* the job at the moment.
5 I was supposed to phone her this morning, but it completely *slipped my mind*.
6 He can't *make up his mind* whether to study medicine or psychology.
7 I went to see the doctor just to *put my mind at rest*.
8 I'm not going to apply for that job at the moment, but I'll *keep it in mind* for the future.
9 I was going to go to the party, but I've *changed my mind* because I don't feel very well.
10 If I had to describe my mother, 'sociable' is something that definitely *springs to mind*.

# Functional Language

## 1 Expressing opinions
Coursebook Unit 1 p9, Unit 5 p54 and Unit 11 p119

I think that …

I don't think that …

I've always thought that …

In my opinion, …

From my point of view, …

As far as I'm concerned, …

I strongly believe that …

I have my doubts about …

## 2 Responding to opinions; agreeeing and disagreeing
Coursebook Unit 2 p21, Unit 9 p96 and Unit 11 p119

| A | I think that it's the best song she's done! |
|---|---|
| B | *Really?* |
| A | In my opinion, bus fares are too expensive. Do you agree? |
| B | *Yes, but* the problem is how to pay for the service. |
| A | I think this town needs a new cinema. |
| B | *True, but* I think a new library is just as important. |
| A | I strongly believe that computers should be available in all schools. |
| B | *Me, too.* |
| A | I think Linda will be late today. |
| B | *Do you? I don't.* She's usually on time. |
| A | I have my doubts about how they are going to cut crime in this area. |
| B | *I know what you mean.* |
| A | I think that the best friends are ones you've known all your life. |
| B | _____ |
| A | As far as I'm concerned, eating a lot of fried food is really bad for you. |
| B | _____ |
| A | I strongly believe that families stick together no matter what happens. |
| B | _____ |

### Agreeing and disagreeing

I totally agree.

I absolutely agree with you.

I agree up to a point, but …

I'm not sure I agree with that.

I don't really agree.

I don't agree at all.

Actually, I disagree with you.

I completely disagree.

### 3 Involving other people/asking for someone else's opinion
Coursebook Unit 12 p128

A *What about you?*
B Well, I completely disagree actually.

A *How about you?*
B I don't really agree.

A So, *what do you think?*
B I'm not sure I completely agree.

A *Do you agree with that?*
B Yes, up to a point.

A *How do you feel about this?*
B I'm not really sure. I can see both sides of the argument.

### 4 Giving yourself 'thinking time' (fillers)
Coursebook Unit 2 p22

Let me see …
Well, I mean …
It depends, really …
I think that depends on various things …
I'm not sure, but I suppose …
I'm not quite sure what I think about that …
I've never thought about that before …
I don't know much about this, but I think …
That's an interesting question …

### 5 Comparing photos
Coursebook Unit 3 p31 and Unit 14 p147
**A Talking about similarities**
*Both pictures are connected to* the theme of entertainment.
*In both pictures, you can see* people playing different kinds of sport.

**B Talking about differences**
In this picture, the place looks quite cold, *whereas* in this one, it is much warmer.
The room in the first picture is very crowded. *In contrast*, the room in the second picture is almost empty.

**C Speculating about the pictures**
*As far as I can tell*, the people in the first picture are teenagers who are at school.
*I'm not sure if* the people in the second picture are at school or not.

**D Giving a personal comment**
*Personally*, I much prefer this kind of film *to* this one.
*I'd rather* live in a place that was quiet *than* somewhere noisy like that.
*I'm not very keen on* dangerous sports like that.

**6 Speculating**

Coursebook Unit 7 p73 and Unit 13 p135

**A The speaker is fairly sure of his/her ideas:**

*There's some kind of* light on a table behind them.

She's wearing *what looks like* rubber boots.

They don't really *look as if* they're enjoying themselves.

They're *probably* police officers – *from* the hats they're wearing.

They *must be* in an exam.

*As far as I can tell*, they *could be* having a meeting.

There is someone who *might be* a computer technician

*I've got a feeling that* they might be friends.

*I think it's more likely that* they are at work.

*I think it's some sort of* machine used in cooking.

*I knew right from the start that* there was something strange going on.

**B The speaker is not sure of his/her ideas:**

They *seem to be* reading something, but *I'm not quite sure why.*

*At first I thought* they were on a train, *but now I'm not so sure.*

*I just can't work out what* the person in the background is doing.

*I don't see how it could be* a child.

*It doesn't make sense.*

**C The speaker is responding directly to someone else's ideas:**

*I hadn't thought of that.*

*I suppose you're right.*

**7 Starting, moving on and finishing a discussion**

Coursebook Unit 13 p136

**Starting the discussion:**

1 *Why don't we start by* talking about healthy exercise?

2 *Shall we* think about what food we like *first*?

3 *Let's begin with* the type of TV programmes.

**Moving the discussion on:**

4 *And what about* the accommodation?

5 *What else do you think is important*?

6 *Let's see. What's left*?

**Finishing the discussion:**

7 *Shall we check that we agree on* what to put first?

8 *So, have we decided which ones* we like best?

9 *Anyway, we have to decide which* three are the most important.

### 8 Justifying choices/giving reasons

Coursebook Unit 14 p143

Linking words followed by a clause:

There's no point in taking any CDs **because** we won't have a CD player there.

**as**

**since**

Linking words followed by a noun phrase:

I don't think he will get the job **because of** his lack of experience.

**due to**

**owing to**

Other phrases/constructions:

- I prefer watching DVDs at home to going to the cinema. *The main reason for this is* that I like to be able to stop the film whenever I like.
- Holidays are very important to me. *If* I have a proper break regularly, *then* I work much more efficiently when I get back.

### 9 Starting and finishing a letter/email

Informal

Coursebook Unit 2 p25 and Unit 8 p84

| Start | Finish |
|---|---|
| *Dear* Mick | *Best wishes* |
| *Hi* Carla | *All the best* |
| *Hello* Jim | *Best* |
| *Hi* | *Love* |
| *Hello* | *Love from* |
| *Hi there!* | *Lots of love* |

Formal

Coursebook Unit 6 p66, Unit 11 p115 and Unit 14 p146

| Start | Finish |
|---|---|
| Dear Mr Smith | Yours sincerely |
| Dear Mrs Evans | |
| Dear Ms Jackson | |
| Dear Miss Breed | |
| Dear Sir | Yours faithfully |
| Dear Madam | |
| Dear Sir/Madam | |

## 10 Organising your ideas
### Coursebook Unit 8 p84

1 *Firstly,* I think that there should be more sports facilities in schools.
2 *First of all, I'd like to say* that traffic jams are a major problem in my town.
3 *The first point is* that students miss out if they do not attend classes regularly.

4 *Secondly,* travelling is a good way of learning about other cultures.
5 *What's more,* it's often easier to learn a language by living in that country.
6 *Another important point is* walking is cheaper than driving.

7 *Finally,* you often get better service in smaller shops.
8 *Last but not least,* you can meet new people by playing different sports.
9 *Then, there is the point about* pollution caused by cars.

## 11 Asking for information
### Coursebook Unit 6 p66
**Neutral/less formal:**

I'd like to know ...
Could you tell me ...?

**More formal:**

I would be (very) grateful if you could tell me ...
I am writing to ask for more information about ...
Could you give me some more information about   ?

## 12 Complaining
### Coursebook Unit 11 p115
**Starting the letter/email**

I am writing to complain about ...
I am writing to express my dissatisfaction with ...

**Explaining the situation**

I was very disappointed by ...
I would like to point out that ...
The advertisement stated that ..., but in fact ...
I was assured that ..., whereas actually ...
When I received the product, to my surprise ...
Even more worrying is the fact that ...

**Saying what you want**

I would like to request that ...
I must insist that you refund my money immediately.
Please can you assure me that you will replace the ... as soon as possible.
I would be grateful if you would give me a refund.

### 13 Comparing ideas
Coursebook Unit 15 p156

1 Young people today have much more freedom *compared with* young people in the past.
2 There's quite a bit more pressure on young people now *in comparison with* a few years ago.
3 Children seem to spend much more time indoors using or playing with technology *unlike* when I was growing up. We were always outside, running around or playing with a ball.
4 *In contrast to* most of her friends, my daughter hates mobile phones.
5 Our teachers encourage us to have our own ideas *as opposed to* just learning other people's opinions off by heart.

### 14 Describing advantages and making recommendations
Coursebook Unit 10 p101

1 More webcams would be *extremely beneficial* as the present facilities are too limited.
2 A new Internet café would *offer many benefits to* the company.
3 *There are a number of good points about* the existing computer suite.
4 A new garden area would be *a valuable addition to* the existing outdoor area.
5 Spending the money on networking the computers would *benefit the company in two main ways.*
6 A DVD player in every classroom *would appeal to many students.*
7 A larger covered patio area *would offer the following advantages.*
8 A new Internet café *would make a big difference to* the school.
9 *I would strongly recommend spending the money on* a new Internet café.

### 15 Overview of linking expressions
Coursebook Unit 12 p129

| Contrast | Addition | Consequence | Conclusion | Purpose |
|---|---|---|---|---|
| although | in addition | because of this | in conclusion | so that |
| whereas | moreover | so | to sum up | in case |
| nevertheless | what's more | therefore | to summarise | to |
| however | as well as | as a result | | so as to |
| despite | furthermore | consequently | | in order to |
| in spite of | not only … but also | due to | | |
| on the other hand | | on account of | | |

# Phrasal Verbs

## 1 Family

1 **to grow up:** *What do you want to be when you grow up?*

2 **to bring (someone) up:** *Her grandparents brought her up.*

3 **to look after:** *I look after my little sister when my mum's at work.*

4 **to look up to (someone):** *I always looked up to my grandfather when I was a child.*

5 **to take after (someone):** *He takes after his father in looks and personality.*

6 **to name (someone) after (someone):** *My parents named me after my mother's mother.*

7 **to live up to (something):** *I found it difficult to live up to my father's high expectations.*

8 **to tell (someone) off:** *My mother always used to tell me off for getting my clothes dirty.*

## 2 Relationships

1 **to get on (with someone):** *I get on with all my flatmates really well.*

2 **to go out with (someone):** *She's been going out with Mick for a year.*

3 **to fall out (with someone):** *I don't think I've ever fallen out with a friend.*

4 **to split up (with someone):** *Jonny and Alison split up after six years of marriage.*

5 **to make up (with someone):** *Have you made up with Daniel yet?*

6 **to let (someone) down:** *I can't trust him because he's let me down so many times.*

7 **to look down on (someone):** *I always feel that my boss is looking down on me.*

8 **to put up with (someone/ something):** *I don't see why I have to put up with your rudeness anymore.*

## 3 Travel

1 **to set off:** *We have to get up early and set off at 6.30 a.m.*

2 **to get on/off:** *Do you know where to get off the bus?*

3 **to pick (someone) up:** *Can you pick me up from the train station?*

4 **to drop (someone) off:** *I'll drop you off at school on my way to work.*

5 **to check in:** *We have to check in two hours before the flight leaves.*

6 **to run out of (something):** *I can't believe we have run out of petrol again.*

7 **to break down:** *I took the bus because my car broke down.*

8 **to take off:** *The worst part of the flight is when the plane takes off.*

## 4 Health

1 **to come down with (something):** *I think I'm coming down with flu.*

2 **to swell up:** *My ankle hurts and it seems to have swollen up.*

3 **to throw up:** *The dog has thrown up all over the carpet.*

4 **to fall over:** *She fell over on the pavement and broke her leg.*

5 **to shake (something) off:** *I can't shake this cold off – I've had it for over a week.*

6 **to pass out:** *The sight of blood made him pass out instantly.*

7 **to pull through:** *He was seriously injured, but I'm sure he'll pull through.*

8 **to pass away:** *I was really upset when my cat passed away last year aged 18.*

### 5 Technology

1 **to turn (something) on/off:**
*Can you turn the light on, please?*

2 **to turn (something) up/down:**
*Let's turn the music up a bit.*

3 **to plug (something) in:** *You can plug the computer in over here.*

4 **to charge (something) up:** *I need to charge my mobile phone up.*

5 **to log in:** *You'll need a password to log in.*

6 **to back (something) up:** *It's really important that you back all your work up every day.*

7 **to print (something) out:** *Can I print this document out on your printer?*

8 **to go off:** *I didn't hear my alarm go off this morning.*

### 6 Learning

1 **to work (something) out:** *I can't work this question out at all.*

2 **to look (something) up:** *Why don't you look it up in a dictionary?*

3 **to fall behind (with something):** *She is lazy and is seriously falling behind with her revision.*

4 **to catch up (with someone/ something):** *It's difficult to catch up with the work if you don't attend all the classes.*

5 **to give/hand (something) in:** *I'd like you to give your essay in on Monday.*

6 **to cross (something) out:** *If you make a mistake, just cross it out.*

7 **to miss (something) out:** *Be sure not to miss any of the questions out.*

8 **to mess (something) up:** *I messed the whole test up because I got the timing wrong.*

> **See also:**
> 10.1 Phrasal verbs (speaking) p12
> 12.2 Phrasal verbs (crime) p15
> 14.2 Phrasal verbs (work) p17

## The Grammar of Phrasal Verbs

**There are four main types of phrasal verbs**

### 1 Verb + adverb (no object)

The verb and the adverb cannot be separated by other words.

*to get on (= to have a good relationship)*
*They aren't **getting on** very well at the moment.*
*They aren't **getting** very well **on** at the moment.*

### 2 Verb + adverb + object (or verb + object + adverb)

The verb and adverb can be separated, but if the object is a pronoun (e.g. *it, me, them*), the adverb must come after the object.

*to make up (= to invent)*
*I think she's **making up** the whole story.*
*I think she's **making** the whole story **up**.*
*I think she's **making** it **up**.*
*I think she's **making up** it.*

### 3 Verb + preposition + object

The verb and preposition cannot be separated.

*to break into (= to enter illegally or by force)*
*They **broke into** our flat and stole the TV and computer.*
*They **broke** our flat **into** and stole the TV and computer.*

### 4 Verb + adverb + preposition + object

The verb, adverb and preposition cannot be separated.

*to put up with (= to tolerate)*
*I don't know how she **puts up with** his terrible behaviour.*
*I don't know how she **puts** his terrible behaviour **up with**.*
*I don't know how she **puts up** his terrible behaviour **with**.*

# Useful Language Chunks

**Write another example for each sentence, using the language chunk in italics.**

**1** We need to leave early because *it takes ages* to get there.

_____.

**2** This coffee machine is *out of order*.

_____.

**3** *There's no point in* talking to him – he won't listen.

_____.

**4** Have you *made arrangements for* the sofa to be delivered?

_____.

**5** She *tried her best* to get here on time, but the train was delayed.

_____.

**6** She *didn't mean to hurt you* – it was an accident.

_____.

**7** *It's a pity* you missed the concert – it was really good fun.

_____.

**8** I'd be grateful if you could all *pay attention to* what I'm saying.

_____.

**9** His name is William but he's *usually known as* Billy.

_____.

**10** He *has difficulty in* concentrating on his studies without being distracted.

_____.

**11** I *last heard from* Julia over three months ago.

_____.

**12** Don't say anything – *it's not worth* arguing about.

_____.

**13** *So far this year*, they've been to five different countries.

_____.

**14** These instructions *don't make sense* – they're very confusing.

_____.

**15** Stonehenge *is said to be* about 3,500 years old.

_____.

**16** I love spending time at the beach – there's *nowhere quite like it.*

_____.

**17** I gave the police *a detailed description* of the person who stole my bag.

_____.

**18** That dog must be more than *double the weight* it should be.

_____.

**19** My parents spend the summer in the mountains *in search of* cooler weather.

_____.

**20** I prefer going shopping *on my own* than going with friends.

_____.

# Top Tips for the Exam

## Reading | Paper 1

**1** Read the text through quickly to get a general idea of the content before doing the detailed questions.

**2** Write an answer for every question, even if you guess. You don't get marks taken off for a wrong answer.

**3** Multiple choice. In part 1 decide what you think the answer is, and *then* look at the four choices.

**4** Gapped text. In part 2 read what comes before and after the gap in the text carefully.

**5** Multiple matching. In part 3 underline key words in the questions and match them with ideas in the text.

## Writing | Paper 2

**1** Plan your time so that you spend an equal amount of time on each question.

**2** Make sure you answer the question in part A (it's compulsory). Then, choose *one* other question from part B.

**3** Write a brief paragraph plan and brainstorm some ideas first.

**4** Leave time to read through what you have written and make any necessary corrections.

**5** Don't waste time counting words. You need to know approximately how much paper your normal handwriting covers using 120–180 words.

## Use of English | Paper 3

**1** Read the text quickly to get a general idea of meaning before filling the gaps (in parts 1, 2 and 3).

**2** Look at the words before and after each gap carefully, checking the grammar and meaning of the missing word (in parts 1, 2 and 3).

**3** Word formation. In part 3 remember that the missing word may need to be plural or negative, it may need a prefix or a suffix added or it may need to change completely (e.g. *long* > *lengthen*).

**4** Key word transformations. In part 4 write between two and five words in the gap including the key word. Don't change the key word.

**5** Write an answer for every question, even if you guess. You don't get marks taken off for a wrong answer.

## Listening | Paper 4

**1** Take time to read through the information and questions before you start listening.

**2** While you're listening for the first time, write the answers on the question paper.

**3** While you're listening for the second time, listen out for key words which justify your answers.

**4** Take the time at the end of the test to copy your answers onto the answer sheet.

**5** Write an answer for every question, even if you guess. You don't get marks taken off for a wrong answer.

## Speaking | Paper 5

**1** Give full, interesting answers including a range of vocabulary and plenty of detail.

**2** Ask the examiner to repeat the question if you don't understand the first time.

**3** Personal information interview. In part 1 make sure you answer the examiner's questions and don't start talking about something else.

**4** Comparing photos. In part 2 don't just describe the photos – do what the examiner asks you.

**5** Collaborative task and Discussion. In parts 3 and 4 make sure you interact with the other candidate by asking for his or her opinion, making suggestions, etc.

# My Exam

## When and where?

| | Date of exam | Time of exam | Place of exam |
|---|---|---|---|
| Paper 1: Reading | | | |
| | | | |
| | | | |
| | | | |
| | | | |

## My revision timetable

- Plan your revision time using the timetable below.
- Don't forget to give yourself rewards including some 'time off'.
- Copy the blank timetable to plan at least ten days of revision.

Day ___ - Date _____

| before 9.00 a.m. | |
|---|---|
| 9.00 a.m. | |
| 10.00 a.m. | |
| 11.00 a.m. | |
| 12.00 a.m. | |
| 1.00 p.m. | |
| 2.00 p.m. | |
| 3.00 p.m. | |
| 4.00 p.m. | |
| 5.00 p.m. | |
| 6.00 p.m. | |
| 7.00 p.m. | |
| 8.00 p.m. | |
| 9.00 p.m. | |
| after 9.00 p.m. | |
| Reward? | |